# DAMN...I'M DEAD.

## The Shit You Need To Know Now That I'm Gone!

### By Mel Caldwell

# TO THE PERSON WHO PURCHASED THIS PLANNER

When my mother died unexpectedly, my mind did not "work" normally. She was my rock. She meant everything to me. All of a sudden, someone that I had known my entire life was suddenly gone. Now, I'm a pretty smart girl, but once the stress and trauma of this loss sunk in, I was a complete ball of emotional mess while trying to find my mother's social security number, bank account information, passwords and information that would be needed for her funeral arrangements.

If my mother had purchased a simple book like the one that you have now, it would have been so much easier for us, as her children, to grieve the shock of her loss, but also plan a funeral that was according to her wishes. My four siblings and I were literally grieving in the dark.

Although my mother was an amazing mother, she had absolutely no life plan. There was no life insurance, savings, cash...nothing. We didn't know anything about planning a funeral, how much it would cost and where to start.

I felt compelled to create this simple book immediately, even while I am still grieving the loss of my mother, because it is my desire to give your loved ones the opportunity to grieve without the pain and frustration of figuring out what they need to do to honor your wishes.

It's time to get your shit together by starting with this book.

# Written by:

_____

# You will find copies of this book located here:

_____

_____

My Signature: _____

| PS: THIS IS NOT A LEGAL DOCUMENT |
|---|

# Table of Contents

. . . . . . . . . . . . . . . . . . . . . . . .

# Before You Read This Journal

. . . . . . . . . . . . . . . . . . . . . . . . . . . .

# Personal Record

· · · · · · · · · · · · · · · · · · · · · · · ·

**Full Name:** _____

**Social Security No.:** _____

**Current Address** _____

_____

**Phone Number(s)** _____

**Email(s):** _____

**Date of Birth:** _____

**Place of Birth:** _____

**Father's Name:** _____

**Mother's Name:** _____

**Social status:**  ☐ Single  ☐ Married  ☐ Divorced
☐ Other: _____

**Spouse:** _____

**Number of children (If any):** _____

**Children's names:** _____
_____
_____
_____

**Brothers:** _____

**Sisters:** _____

**Financial status:**  ☐ Employed  ☐ Unemployed
☐ Entrepreneur  ☐ Small business owner
☐ Other: _____

# Important Contacts

. . . . . . . . . . . . . . . . . . . . . . . . . . .

## Attorneys:

Name: ——————————————————————————

Phone: ——————————————————————————

Email: ——————————————————————————

Address: ——————————————————————————


Name: ——————————————————————————

Phone: ——————————————————————————

Email: ——————————————————————————

Address: ——————————————————————————


Name: ——————————————————————————

Phone: ——————————————————————————

Email: ——————————————————————————

Address: ——————————————————————————

# Important Contacts

· · · · · · · · · · · · · · · · · · · · · · · · ·

## Doctors:

Name: ————————————————————————

Phone: ————————————————————————

Email: ————————————————————————

Address: ——————————————————————


Name: ————————————————————————

Phone: ————————————————————————

Email: ————————————————————————

Address: ——————————————————————


Name: ————————————————————————

Phone: ————————————————————————

Email: ————————————————————————

Address: ——————————————————————

# Important Contacts

. . . . . . . . . . . . . . . . . . . . . . . . .

## Relatives:

Name: _____

Phone: _____

Email: _____

Address: _____


Name: _____

Phone: _____

Email: _____

Address: _____


Name: _____

Phone: _____

Email: _____

Address: _____

# Important Contacts

· · · · · · · · · · · · · · · · · · · · · · · ·

## Relatives:

Name: _____

Phone: _____

Email: _____

Address: _____

Name: _____

Phone: _____

Email: _____

Address: _____

Name: _____

Phone: _____

Email: _____

Address: _____

# Important Contacts

. . . . . . . . . . . . . . . . . . . . . . . . . .

## Relatives:

Name: _____

Phone: _____

Email: _____

Address: _____

Name: _____

Phone: _____

Email: _____

Address: _____

Name: _____

Phone: _____

Email: _____

Address: _____

# Important Contacts

· · · · · · · · · · · · · · · · · · · · · · · · ·

## Relatives:

Name: ——————————————————————————

Phone: ——————————————————————————

Email: ——————————————————————————

Address: ——————————————————————————

Name: ——————————————————————————

Phone: ——————————————————————————

Email: ——————————————————————————

Address: ——————————————————————————

Name: ——————————————————————————

Phone: ——————————————————————————

Email: ——————————————————————————

Address: ——————————————————————————

# Important Contacts

. . . . . . . . . . . . . . . . . . . . . . . .

## Relatives:

Name: _____

Phone: _____

Email: _____

Address: _____


Name: _____

Phone: _____

Email: _____

Address: _____


Name: _____

Phone: _____

Email: _____

Address: _____

# Important Contacts

· · · · · · · · · · · · · · · · · · · · · · · · · · ·

## Relatives:

Name: _____

Phone: _____

Email: _____

Address: _____

Name: _____

Phone: _____

Email: _____

Address: _____

Name: _____

Phone: _____

Email: _____

Address: _____

# Important Contacts

· · · · · · · · · · · · · · · · · · · · · · · ·

## Friends:

Name: ─────────────────────────────────

Phone: ─────────────────────────────────

Email: ─────────────────────────────────

Address: ───────────────────────────────

Name: ─────────────────────────────────

Phone: ─────────────────────────────────

Email: ─────────────────────────────────

Address: ───────────────────────────────

Name: ─────────────────────────────────

Phone: ─────────────────────────────────

Email: ─────────────────────────────────

Address: ───────────────────────────────

# Important Contacts

............................

## Friends:

Name: _____

Phone: _____

Email: _____

Address: _____


Name: _____

Phone: _____

Email: _____

Address: _____


Name: _____

Phone: _____

Email: _____

Address: _____

# Important Contacts

.............................

## Friends:

Name: _____

Phone: _____

Email: _____

Address: _____


Name: _____

Phone: _____

Email: _____

Address: _____


Name: _____

Phone: _____

Email: _____

Address: _____

# Important Contacts

. . . . . . . . . . . . . . . . . . . . . . . . . . .

## Friends:

Name: _____

Phone: _____

Email: _____

Address: _____

Name: _____

Phone: _____

Email: _____

Address: _____

Name: _____

Phone: _____

Email: _____

Address: _____

# Important Contacts

. . . . . . . . . . . . . . . . . . . . . . . . .

## Friends:

Name: _____

Phone: _____

Email: _____

Address: _____


Name: _____

Phone: _____

Email: _____

Address: _____


Name: _____

Phone: _____

Email: _____

Address: _____

# Important Contacts

## Others.....................

Name: _____

Phone: _____

Email: _____

Address: _____


Name: _____

Phone: _____

Email: _____

Address: _____


Name: _____

Phone: _____

Email: _____

Address: _____

# Important Contacts

## Others.....................

Name: _____

Phone: _____

Email: _____

Address: _____


Name: _____

Phone: _____

Email: _____

Address: _____


Name: _____

Phone: _____

Email: _____

Address: _____

# Important Contacts

## Others.....................

Name: _____

Phone: _____

Email: _____

Address: _____


Name: _____

Phone: _____

Email: _____

Address: _____


Name: _____

Phone: _____

Email: _____

Address: _____

# Important Contacts

## Others.....................

Name: _____

Phone: _____

Email: _____

Address: _____


Name: _____

Phone: _____

Email: _____

Address: _____


Name: _____

Phone: _____

Email: _____

Address: _____

# Important Contacts

## Others.....................

Name: _____

Phone: _____

Email: _____

Address: _____


Name: _____

Phone: _____

Email: _____

Address: _____


Name: _____

Phone: _____

Email: _____

Address: _____

# Important Contacts

## Others.....................

Name: ———————————————————————————————

Phone: ———————————————————————————————

Email: ———————————————————————————————

Address: ———————————————————————————————

Name: ———————————————————————————————

Phone: ———————————————————————————————

Email: ———————————————————————————————

Address: ———————————————————————————————

Name: ———————————————————————————————

Phone: ———————————————————————————————

Email: ———————————————————————————————

Address: ———————————————————————————————

# Important Documents

............................

Document: _____

Location: _____

What to do: _____

_____

_____


Document: _____

Location: _____

What to do: _____

_____

_____


Document: _____

Location: _____

What to do: _____

_____

_____

# Important Documents

· · · · · · · · · · · · · · · · · · · · · · · · · ·

Document: _____

Location: _____

What to do: _____

_____

_____

_____


Document: _____

Location: _____

What to do: _____

_____

_____


Document: _____

Location: _____

What to do: _____

_____

_____

# Important Documents

. . . . . . . . . . . . . . . . . . . . . . . . . .

Document: _____

Location: _____

What to do: _____

_____

_____

_____

Document: _____

Location: _____

What to do: _____

_____

_____

Document: _____

Location: _____

What to do: _____

_____

_____

# Important Documents

. . . . . . . . . . . . . . . . . . . . . . . . . .

Document: _____

Location: _____

What to do: _____

_____

_____

Document: _____

Location: _____

What to do: _____

_____

Document: _____

Location: _____

What to do: _____

_____

_____

# My Properties

∙∙∙∙∙∙∙∙∙∙∙∙∙∙∙∙∙∙∙∙∙∙∙∙∙

Type: _____

Location: _____

_____

Co-owner(s): _____

Year of acquisition: _____


Type: _____

Location: _____

_____

Co-owner(s): _____

Year of acquisition: _____

# My Properties

························

Type: _____

Location: _____

_____

Co-owner(s): _____

Year of acquisition: _____


Type: _____

Location: _____

_____

Co-owner(s): _____

Year of acquisition: _____

# My Properties

· · · · · · · · · · · · · · · · · · · · · · · ·

Type: _____

Location: _____

_____

Co-owner(s): _____

Year of acquisition: _____


Type: _____

Location: _____

_____

Co-owner(s): _____

Year of acquisition: _____

# Financial Information

## Bank Accounts & Credit Cards

Account number: _____

Account holder name: _____

Credit card type:  ☐ **Visa**   ☐ **Mastercard**   ☐ **American Express**

☐ **Other:** _____

Card user name: _____

Card password: _____

Expiration date: _____


Account number: _____

Account holder name: _____

Credit card type:  ☐ **Visa**   ☐ **Mastercard**   ☐ **American Express**

☐ **Other:** _____

Card user name: _____

Card password: _____

Expiration date: _____

# Financial Information

## Bank Accounts & Credit Cards

Account number: _____

Account holder name: _____

Credit card type:  ☐ Visa   ☐ Mastercard   ☐ American Express

☐ Other: _____

Card user name: _____

Card password: _____

Expiration date: _____


Account number: _____

Account holder name: _____

Credit card type:  ☐ Visa   ☐ Mastercard   ☐ American Express

☐ Other: _____

Card user name: _____

Card password: _____

Expiration date: _____

# Financial Information

## Bank Accounts & Credit Cards

Account number: _____

Account holder name: _____

Credit card type: ☐ Visa ☐ Mastercard ☐ American Express

☐ Other: _____

Card user name: _____

Card password: _____

Expiration date: _____


Account number: _____

Account holder name: _____

Credit card type: ☐ Visa ☐ Mastercard ☐ American Express

☐ Other: _____

Card user name: _____

Card password: _____

Expiration date: _____

# Financial Information

## Bank Accounts & Credit Cards

Account number: _____

Account holder name: _____

Credit card type: ☐ **Visa**  ☐ **Mastercard**  ☐ **American Express**

☐ **Other:** _____

Card user name: _____

Card password: _____

Expiration date: _____


Account number: _____

Account holder name: _____

Credit card type: ☐ **Visa**  ☐ **Mastercard**  ☐ **American Express**

☐ **Other:** _____

Card user name: _____

Card password: _____

Expiration date: _____

# Financial Information

## Bank Accounts & Credit Cards

Account number: _____

Account holder name: _____

Credit card type: ☐ Visa ☐ Mastercard ☐ American Express

☐ Other: _____

Card user name: _____

Card password: _____

Expiration date: _____


Account number: _____

Account holder name: _____

Credit card type: ☐ Visa ☐ Mastercard ☐ American Express

☐ Other: _____

Card user name: _____

Card password: _____

Expiration date: _____

# Financial Information

## Safe Deposit Boxes

Number: _____

Address or location: _____

Date opened: _____

Period of engagement: _____


Number: _____

Address or location: _____

Date opened: _____

Period of engagement: _____


Number: _____

Address or location: _____

Date opened: _____

Period of engagement: _____

# Financial Information

## Others:

# Financial Information

## Others:

_____

_____

_____

_____

_____

_____

_____

_____

_____

_____

_____

_____

# Financial Information

## Others:

_____

_____

_____

_____

_____

_____

_____

_____

_____

_____

_____

_____

_____

# Financial Information

## Others:

_____

_____

_____

_____

_____

_____

_____

_____

_____

_____

_____

_____

# Insurance Information

Insurance type: _____

Company/Agency: _____

Agent: _____

Phone: _____

Email: _____

Notes: _____
_____
_____
_____

Insurance type: _____

Company/Agency: _____

Agent: _____

Phone: _____

Email: _____

Notes: _____
_____
_____
_____

# Insurance Information

Insurance type: _____

Company/Agency: _____

Agent: _____

Phone: _____

Email: _____

Notes: _____
_____
_____
_____

Insurance type: _____

Company/Agency: _____

Agent: _____

Phone: _____

Email: _____

Notes: _____
_____
_____
_____

# Insurance Information

· · · · · · · · · · · · · · · · · · · · · · · · · · ·

Insurance type: _____

Company/Agency: _____

Agent: _____

Phone: _____

Email: _____

Notes: _____
_____
_____
_____

Insurance type: _____

Company/Agency: _____

Agent: _____

Phone: _____

Email: _____

Notes: _____
_____
_____

# Insurance Information

· · · · · · · · · · · · · · · · · · · · · · · · · ·

Insurance type: _____

Company/Agency: _____

Agent: _____

Phone: _____

Email: _____

Notes: _____
_____
_____
_____

Insurance type: _____

Company/Agency: _____

Agent: _____

Phone: _____

Email: _____

Notes: _____
_____
_____
_____

# Internet Accounts, Emails, Profiles, and Social Media...

Email: ———————————— Password: ——————

Email: ———————————— Password: ——————

Email: ———————————— Password: ——————

Email: ———————————— Password: ——————


FB account: ————————— Password: ——————

FB account: ————————— Password: ——————

FB account: ————————— Password: ——————


Instagram account: ———— Password: ——————

Instagram account: ———— Password: ——————

Instagram account: ———— Password: ——————


Twitter account: ————— Password: ——————

Twitter account: ————— Password: ——————

Twitter account: ————— Password: ——————

# Internet Accounts, Emails, Profiles, and Social Media...

Email: ——————————— Password: ———————

Email: ——————————— Password: ———————

Email: ——————————— Password: ———————

Email: ——————————— Password: ———————


FB account: ——————————— Password: ———————

FB account: ——————————— Password: ———————

FB account: ——————————— Password: ———————


Instagram account: ——————— Password: ———————

Instagram account: ——————— Password: ———————

Instagram account: ——————— Password: ———————


Twitter account: ——————— Password: ———————

Twitter account: ——————— Password: ———————

Twitter account: ——————— Password: ———————

# My Wishes

# My Wishes For My Spouse

. . . . . . . . . . . . . . . . . . . . . . . . . . .

# My Wishes For My Children

. . . . . . . . . . . . . . . . . . . . . . . . . . .

# My Wishes For My Relatives

. . . . . . . . . . . . . . . . . . . . . . . . . . . .

# My Wishes For My Friends & Colleagues

. . . . . . . . . . . . . . . . . . . . . . . . . . . .

# My Wishes For My Pets

. . . . . . . . . . . . . . . . . . . . . . . . . . .

# My Letters

# Letter to:...................

# Letter to:………………

# Letter to:...................

# Letter to:………………

# Letter to:………………

# Letter to:………………

# Letter to:...................

# Letter to:...................

# My
# Apologies

# My Apologies

· · · · · · · · · · · · · · · · · · · · · · · · · ·

# My Apologies

· · · · · · · · · · · · · · · · · · · · · · · · ·

# My Apologies

· · · · · · · · · · · · · · · · · · · · · · · · · ·

# My Apologies

· · · · · · · · · · · · · · · · · · · · · · · · ·

# My Apologies

# Recommendations For My Funeral

This section may feel very uncomfortable to fill out at first, but if you can do it, it will be extremely helpful to your loved ones when planning your funeral.

Burial or Cremation:_____

Funeral Home:_____

Officiant:_____

Scriptures to use:_____

_____

_____

Song selections:_____

_____

_____

Reading of Obituary:_____

Eulogist:_____

People who I would like to give remarks:

_____

_____

_____

# Other notes pertaining to your funeral wishes...

# My Last Words

# Extra Notes

Made in United States
North Haven, CT
18 October 2024

59088877R10059